P9-CAL-454
'RY

"BASEBALL IS JUST BASEBALL"
THE UNDERSTATED ICHIRO

An unauthorized collection compiled by David Shields

© 2001 TNI Books
All rights reserved.

Except for appropriate use in critical reviews or works of
scholarship, the reproduction or use of this work in any form or
by any electronic, mechanical, or other means now known or
hereafter invented, including photocopying and recording, and
in any information storage and retrieval system is forbidden
without the written permission of the publisher.

The quotations in this book are reproduced from interviews
with and stories about Ichiro Suzuki.

International Standard Book Number: 0-9678703-1-3

Design by Chris Pew @ Capsule9
capsule9.com

Cover illustration by James Hunt
crimsonghost.com

TNI Books
2442 NW Market #357
Seattle WA 98107
tnibooks@tnibooks.com
tnibooks.com

David Shields is the author of five previous books of fiction and
nonfiction, including, most recently, *Black Planet*, which was a
finalist for the National Book Critics Circle Award.

Visit David Shields online
davidshields.com

Printed in Canada by Westcan Printing Group
westcanpg.com

INTRODUCTION

I agonized all spring about whether to get cable TV. I didn't want my eight-year-old daughter, Natalie, to get hooked on the Cartoon Network, but I wanted to watch the Mariners, who were off to a brilliant start – not just winning the overwhelming majority of their games, but playing a new (for them), beautiful brand of team baseball: sacrifice bunts rather than three-run homers. I went so far as to call the cable company, get estimates for packages, and two times scheduled appointments for installation, only to cancel both times.

A week and a half into the season, I was listening to the A's – Mariners game on the radio; after a few innings, I couldn't stand it any longer and, though I don't drink, I ran around the corner to a sports bar. Oakland's Terrence Long was on first base. The next batter singled to right field, and when Long tried to run from first to third base (a relatively routine maneuver), the Mariners' right-fielder, Ichiro Suzuki – the first Japanese position-player in the major leagues and who, like Madonna or Cher or Pelé, went only by his first name – threw the ball on a low line-drive from medium-deep right field all the way to the third baseman, who easily tagged Long out.

The bar erupted, the announcer went berserk, I felt that weird tingle down my spine I get about twice a decade, and for the next twenty-four hours all anyone could talk about – on the post-game show, on sports-talk radio, on the pre-game show the next day – was "The Throw." Several players, coaches, and broadcasters said it was the single greatest throw they'd ever seen.

"The ball came out of a cannon; it was quick and powerful."

"It was like Ichiro threw a coin to third base."

"He threw a laser."

"It was like something out of *Star Wars*."

Even Terrence Long said, "It was going to take a perfect throw to get me, and it was a perfect throw."

4

Asked to explain, Ichiro said, "The ball was hit right to me. Why did he run when I was going to throw him out?"

Cable was installed by the end of the week. Day after day a similar scenario would play out on the diamond. Ichiro would perform some Herculean feat on the field — an amazing throw or catch or steal or hit — and then afterward, asked about it, he'd say something that was... surprising. He'd dismiss it or deny it or demur or empty out the premise or give credit elsewhere. Now that I had cable, I decided to supplement my subscription to the *Seattle Times* with a subscription to the *Seattle Post-Intelligencer*. I couldn't wait to get up every morning and, while I ate my breakfast and made Natalie's lunch (and while she watched the Cartoon Network), read what Ichiro said today about what he'd done last night. He never boasted in the way I was accustomed to athletes doing, or if he did, he seemed to do so in a way that was fresh and funny in its uncluttered assertion of neutral fact.

Was I making too much of this? Was I trying to impart philosophic significance to simple athletic excellence? Maybe the words acquired a lyrical glamour as they got translated from Japanese to English? Perhaps it was the translators themselves who were turning Ichiro's ordinary statements into haunting aphorisms? Maybe it was a cultural-transmission issue: maybe what were to my Western ears Zen koans were, to Ichiro, self-evident truths, the only gestures available? I could analyze it to death, but I'd rather not. I'd prefer instead to encourage you to take a few minutes out and read Ichiro's sayings and naysayings. I hope you find them as provocative and inspiring as I do.

David Shields
Seattle, 2001

ASSOCIATED PRESS, April 12, 2001;
MARINERS BROADCASTS ON KIRO, April 11 and 12, 2001

PERSONAL (VITAL):

Ichiro Suzuki was born October 22, 1973 in Kasugai, Japan. He is 5'10",
weighs 160 pounds, plays right field, throws right, bats left, and runs from
home plate to first base in 3.7 seconds. Ichiro spent his childhood in
Kasugai (pop. 266,000), a suburb of Nagoya, attended Aiko-Dai Meiden
High School, and married Yumiko Fukushima, a 34-year-old former
Japanese news personality.

PERSONAL (ODD FACTS):

The name "Ichiro" means "number one son," although Ichiro was actually
the second-born son in his family. He started going only by his first name
because his team, the Orix Blue Wave, already had three other players with
the surname of Suzuki. According to a recent poll, Ichiro is the most
recognizable person in Japan (the Emperor came in a distant second).
Ichiro doesn't drink, loves to play golf, and enjoys hip-hop music. He gets
his gloves custom-made – 3 per year – by legendary Japanese glove maker
Yoshi Tsubota.

MAJOR LEAGUE BASEBALL (AS OF 2001 SEASON ALL-STAR BREAK):

At the All-Star break in his rookie season in Major League Baseball, Ichiro
was third in the league in batting average (.347), first in hits (134) and
runs (76), tied for first in stolen bases (28), second in triples (7), and had
41 RBI and 5 HR. He has had hitting streaks of 23 and 15 games.

The Seattle Mariners paid the Orix Blue Wave $13.1 million for the right to
negotiate with Ichiro, who on November 18 2000, signed a three-year, $14
million dollar contract, becoming the first position-player from Japan to
play in the major leagues. He is the first rookie ever to draw the most
overall votes for the All-Star Game (3,373,035). His first hit of the season
came in the first game of the year on April 2 in the 7th inning off Oakland
A's reliever T.J. Matthews. Ichiro was named the American League Rookie
of the Month in April and May.

JAPAN:

In Japan, Ichiro's career totals are a .353 batting average, 1,278 hits, 658 runs, 199 stolen bases, 118 HR, and 529 RBI. In 2000, he won his seventh straight batting title, led the league in on-base percentage for the fifth time in his career with a .460 mark, was named to his seventh straight All-Star team, and won his seventh consecutive Gold Glove Award. In 1997, he went a Japanese-record 216 plate appearances without striking out from April 16 to June 25. In 1996, he was named Pacific League MVP for the third consecutive year and appeared in one game as a pitcher (in high school, his fast ball had been clocked at 93 mph). In 1994, Ichiro won his first league batting title, hitting .385 with 13 HR and 54 RBI, setting a league record with 210 hits in just 130 games. In 1993, he hit .371 with eight home runs in 48 games in the minors and hit .188 in 64 at-bats with the major-league Blue Wave. On June 12, he hit his first professional home run off the Kinetsu Buffaloes' Hideo Nomo. In 1991, he was selected by the Orix Blue Wave in the fourth round of the Japanese draft.

A reporter asked Ichiro if he ever thought he'd be where he is in his first season — on pace to break the major-league record for the most number of hits in a season. Ichiro replied, **"When I came here to play, I didn't know where I would be or where I wouldn't be."**

ASSOCIATED PRESS, June 11 2001

Six weeks into the season, Ichiro had two or more hits in seven games. Asked whether this was surprising, he said, **"It's somewhere between usual and surprising."**

SEATTLE POST-INTELLIGENCER, May 19 2001

When a reporter pointed out to Ichiro that he was batting .625 with runners in scoring position and less than two outs, Ichiro replied, **"I didn't know I hit that way. Maybe not knowing is my secret. If I chased numbers, maybe I wouldn't have as good results."**

SEATTLE TIMES, May 16 2001

No one approached Ichiro for an autograph while he strolled the streets outside his hotel in Minneapolis. Asked if people are surprised by his size (5'9", 160 pounds) or simply don't recognize him, he said, **"I'm told I either look bigger than I do on television or that I look smaller than I look on television. No one seems to think I look the same size."**

TACOMA NEWS TRIBUNE, May 23 2001

Most players have only one swing and try to swing at a ball only in the strike zone. Ichiro has at least five different swings, and he appears to swing at the ball regardless of where it's pitched, often lunging at it. Asked to explain his unorthodox approach, he said, **"It works for me."**

KANSAS CITY STAR, May 27 2001

Asked to explain the purpose of the ritual he performs before every pitch – swinging the bat over his head clockwise, pointing his right arm directly at the pitcher, stretching his left arm, bending his elbow to touch his right shoulder and tug on his uniform, holding that position, then releasing and cocking the bat to hit – Ichiro said, **"Some people may think it's strange, but if something works, there's no need to change it."**

SPORTS ILLUSTRATED, May 28 2001

Congratulated on getting a hit his first at-bat in spring training, Ichiro said, **"That wasn't a hit. That was some bad fielding by the pitcher."**

SEATTLE TIMES, March 2 2001

Mariners CEO Howard Lincoln said, "Ichiro is not just the most popular baseball player in Japan. He's one of the most popular people. He's a combination of baseball star and rock star. Every single thing about him is followed very closely." Ichiro's agent, Tony Attanasio, said, "It's fanaticism. You can't have a dinner at a restaurant unless it's in a guarded private room. Otherwise, it would be impossible for him to eat." Asked to talk about what a relief it must be for him to be in America and not be as inundated by media as he was in Japan, Ichiro said, **"It's nice to be able to get out for dinner with my wife and have some private time in public places, but I think the American media has the misconception that I was swarmed by hundreds of people wherever I went in Japan. That just wasn't the case."**

SPORTING NEWS, February 20 2001;
SEATTLE TIMES, March 30 2001;
ASAHI SHIMBUN, May 8 2001

Asked if he feels anxiety about the prospect of living abroad in Seattle, Ichiro answered, **"I still can't speak English, and there's a lot of pressure. There are a lot of things to worry about, unexpected things, because the mentality and the manners are different. Even if there are things that become somewhat stressful, I think they're interesting. Isn't it because of those things that I am able to be struck by the significance of being alive?"**

ICHIRO AND THE INTERVIEW: ATTACK THE PINNACLE!, April 2001

Ichiro said about the spacious Safeco Field, **"The best way to approach this park is to hit for extra bases. I don't think I can hit home runs with these skinny arms."**

SEATTLE TIMES, November 30 2000

Asked if he was surprised by the greater velocity of American pitchers, Ichiro said, **"There have been no surprises."**

SEATTLE TIMES, March 8 2001

Asked if it was a problem to adjust to the wider
strike zone in the United States, Ichiro said,
"I would not want to address this as a problem."

SEATTLE TIMES, March 30 2001

Asked about adjusting to the wider major-league strike zone, Ichiro said, **"I don't see any problems adjusting to the strike zone in America."**

SEATTLE TIMES, March 30 2001

Ichiro said, **"The players, especially the catchers, don't argue with the umpires or show any negative body language like they do in Japan. They just don't argue the way they do in Japan."** Asked why he hasn't gotten into any arguments with major-league umpires, he said, **"So far nothing has bothered me."**

MLB.com, May 30 2001

A month into the season, Ichiro declined to be
interviewed for or pose for a *Sports Illustrated*
cover article, saying, **"I haven't done anything yet."**

JAPAN ECONOMIC NEWSWIRE, May 10 2001

Asked how his winter training was going in preparation for his first year in the major leagues, Ichiro said, **"At this time of the year it all feels the same, good or bad."**

JAPAN TIMES, January 8 2001

Lou Piniella said about Ichiro, "He's like Lewis and Clark. I don't think Ichiro knows who Lewis and Clark were, though." Ichiro said, **"People say I'm an explorer, a pioneer, whatever. That's other people's opinion. That's not why I came over here. I came over here to play baseball."**

SEATTLE TIMES, March 30 2001;
SEATTLE POST-INTELLIGENCER, March 30 2001

At the beginning of the season, asked what he thought about the historical significance of what he was doing, Ichiro said, **"I don't think about history – not now. Maybe I'll think about history at the end of the year. Maybe not until years from now."**

SEATTLE TIMES, June 7 2001

When he was asked to talk about any special feelings he might have after playing his first "official" spring-training game with the Mariners, Ichiro said, **"I apologize, but today was just another game to me. I know it has some importance to the media, but not to me. Even being the first game, I was excited, not anxious. The most exciting thing that happened to me was getting through the media interviews after the game."**

SEATTLE TIMES, March 2 2001

Asked to comment about hitting his second home
run of spring training, Ichiro's only response
was: **"It was a hit-and-run."**

SEATTLE TIMES, March 24 2001

Mayor Paul Schell declared April 1st Ichiro Suzuki Day; on the following day, Opening Day featured elaborate pre-game ceremonies honoring Ichiro and the Mariners, and the "historic ball" with which Ichiro got his first hit was taken out of the game. Asked for his reaction to all the fanfare, Ichiro said, **"Of course, I'm glad to have this day over with. Now I must start thinking about tomorrow."**

SEATTLE TIMES, April 3 2001

The Mariners played back-to-back series against San Diego and Oakland. A broadcaster asked Ichiro if he had any reaction to playing in the cities in which two of the greatest major-league hitters grew up – Ted Williams (who grew up in San Diego) and Joe DiMaggio (who actually grew up in San Francisco). Ichiro said, **"American players probably have stronger feelings toward those other players. I've heard those names a lot, but I've never seen them play on the field."**

"MARINER TALK" ON KIRO, June 18 2001

Asked what he thought his main contributions
to the Mariners would be, Ichiro said,
**"Hitting, throwing, speed, and balance. That's
what I'm good at."**

JAPAN TIMES, January 18 2001

A number of players said that Ichiro was getting hit by a lot of pitches because he's a "diver" — someone who leans into the ball and therefore is vulnerable to being hit by inside pitches. The Chicago White Sox star Frank Thomas said, "He's a slap hitter. That's his game. He dives a lot, and that's going to be a problem for him, because guys here will knock him off the plate. Pitchers in the American League try to establish the inner part of the plate." Asked for his response, Ichiro said, **"I don't think I do that."**

SEATTLE POST-INTELLIGENCER, March 15 2001

Piniella suggested to Ichiro that he take a day off.
Ichiro declined, saying, **"Why?"**

"DAVE MAHLER SHOW" ON KJR, June 22 2001

33

According to injured Mariner outfielder Jay Buhner, who is a home-run hitter and whose position Ichiro has taken, "The little shit can hit one bomb after another in batting practice, but in a game he'll only let it fly in certain situations." Asked why he rarely hits home runs during the game, Ichiro said, **"I'm planning to turn on the power after the All-Star break."**

ESPN THE MAGAZINE, May 14 2001;
BROADCAST OF MARINERS GAME ON KIRO, June 9 2001

The Mariners' designated hitter Edgar Martinez was injured and unable to play, so Mariners coach John McLaren told Ichiro that he would be the DH that night. Asked if he was surprised, Ichiro said, **"It was a surprise, but not a huge surprise. If he told me I was going to pitch, that would be a bigger surprise."**

SEATTLE POST-INTELLIGENCER, June 4 2001

The Chicken came onto the field between the first and second innings and bantered with Ichiro. Coming off the field, The Chicken fell down the dugout steps. Asked his reaction to The Chicken, Ichiro said, **"I hoped he was okay."**

SEATTLE TIMES, May 28 2001

Referring to the fact that Ken Griffey, Jr., decided not to return to the Mariners after the 1999 season, Ichiro said, **"When I left Arizona in 1999, Griffey gave me a bat signed, 'See you in Seattle,' so it seems he lied to me."**

SEATTLE TIMES, January 23 2001

Asked about being hit by a pitch twice in one game, Ichiro said, **"Everybody seems to have a different approach on how to pitch me. It's never the same."**

ASSOCIATED PRESS, May 14 2001

Asked why, when he stole third base, he didn't slide, Ichiro said, **"I didn't think he [the catcher] would throw."**

SEATTLE POST-INTELLIGENCER, May 4 2001

As he does after every game, Ichiro rubbed a
6-inch wooden stick up and down the sides and
bottoms of his feet, massaging the pressure
points. Asked the name of the device he was
using, Ichiro said, **"Wood."**

ASSOCIATED PRESS, May 22 2001

Asked why he massages his feet, he said, **"If your feet are healthy, you're healthy."**

SPORTS ILLUSTRATED, May 28 2001

Ichiro, responding to a rumor that a Japanese magazine was offering $1 million for a nude photo of him, said, **"If that was true, I'd take the picture myself and send it in."**

WASHINGTON POST, April 29 2001

Ichiro was asked how much a magazine would have to pay him to pose nude. **"I'd do it if they'd disappear,"** he said. You mean, he was asked, you'd do it if they'd stop following you? **"I'd do it if they'd disappear from the planet,"** he replied.

ESPNMAG.COM, May 7 2001

Ichiro was asked what superpower would he most want – the strength of 100 men, the ability to fly, or the ability to turn invisible? **"Invisible,"** he replied. **"I could go anywhere and see anything without telling anybody."**

ESPNMAG.COM, May 7 2001

Asked how he felt after his first spring-training game with the Mariners in 1999, Ichiro said, **"It felt good: it was a brand-new feeling that I hadn't felt before."**

KYODO NEWS SERVICE, March 4 1999

Asked, before the season started, what he thought major-league baseball would be like, Ichiro replied, **"I have no idea what it's going to be like playing in the majors this year. I can only imagine what it might be like, so I'll just have to experience it."**

JAPAN TIMES, January 8 2001

Asked how he thought he'd be affected by the grind of the major-league season, which is 32 games longer than the Japanese season, Ichiro said, **"I can't say how it will affect me, because I've never experienced it before."**

ASAHI SHIMBUN, May 8 2001

Discussing why he wanted to attend spring training in the United States while he was still under contract with a Japanese team, Ichiro said, **"Sometimes you just have to physically try things out."**

KYODO NEWS SERVICE, March 8 1999

In a game against the Baltimore Orioles, Ichiro made two spectacular diving catches. Orioles manager Mike Hargrove said, "The catch he made on Anderson's ball down the line and the catch he made on Hairston's ball – no other right fielder in the American League makes those plays. Maybe he makes one of them, but doesn't make both of them." Asked, afterward, which of the catches was the most difficult, Ichiro said, **"It's tough to say which one was the toughest, because each fly ball had a different characteristic."**

BALTIMORE SUN, May 31 2001

Ichiro expressed disappointment that he hadn't caught a ball that went just over his glove. **"If I had jumped like Michael Jordan, I could have caught the home run,"** Ichiro said, **"but I don't have the same jump."**

ASSOCIATED PRESS, May 19 2001

Ichiro reached high above the wall, caught what otherwise would have been a home run, fell to the ground, did a backwards somersault, adjusted his sunglasses, and then slowly pulled the ball out from under his glove to show that he had caught it. Asked to analyze the play, he said, **"It was a fly ball; I caught it."**

SEATTLE POST-INTELLIGENCER, May 29 2001

During a game between the Mariners and A's in Oakland, fans in the right-field bleachers taunted him with racial epithets and threw quarters and ice at him. A man who hit Ichiro in the head with a quarter stood and took a bow. Afterward, asked what happened, Ichiro said – according to the translator, Ted Heid – **"Something came out of the stands and hit me."** Ichiro immediately said something to Heid, who said, "I must correct my previous interpretation. Ichiro said, **'Something came out of the sky and hit me.'"** Asked how much money he collected, Ichiro said, **"I couldn't tell if it was rain or money coming down."** Asked if something like this had ever happened to him in Japan, he said, **"Of course it happened there. Any time you come in as a visiting team, things fall out of the sky. The gods once threw an aluminum can at me."**

SEATTLE TIMES, April 12 2001

Asked his reaction to Alex Rodriguez getting booed so vociferously upon his return to Seattle, Ichiro said, **"It's very tough for a ballplayer to get proud and keep his dignity. There's not much difference between love and hate."**

BASEBALLPROSPECTUS.COM, April 22 2001

Asked which is the worst mascot, the Mariners
Moose or the Orix Blue Wave Neppie [the
sea-creature mascot of his former team in Japan],
Ichiro said, **"I like them both."**

ESPNMAG.COM, May 7 2001

Discussing differences between Japanese and American fans, Ichiro said, **"Here they cheer for both teams, not just the home team. I like that."**

SEATTLE POST-INTELLIGENCER, March 30 2001

Asked how it felt to be greeted warmly by Japanese fans in every city the Mariners visited, Ichiro said, **"There are many Japanese people living in the cities we have played and they're welcoming me. At the same time, they're die-hard fans for their home team, so it's kind of a mixture of fans who want to see me do well, but also want their team to win the game."**

MLB.com, May 30 2001

In a game against Minnesota, Ichiro singled. When Ichiro arrived at first base, the Twins' muscular, home-run-hitting first-baseman Doug Mientkiewicz said to Ichiro, **"I wish I had your legs,"** to which Ichiro replied, **"I wish I had your swing."**

SEATTLE TIMES, May 24 2001

Before an exhibition game, Ichiro met Mark McGwire, who set a major-league record with 70 home runs two seasons ago. McGwire said, **"I wish I had some of your speed."** Ichiro said, **"I wish I had some of your upper-body strength."**

SEATTLE POST-INTELLIGENCER, April 2 2001

When he was given number 51 to wear, Ichiro said, **"I'm very fortunate the Mariners would let me wear 51, and I'll work hard not to damage the reputation of the number, because Randy Johnson was a fine pitcher for Seattle for many years."**

SEATTLE POST-INTELLIGENCER, March 14 2001

Asked at the beginning of the year what sort of adjustments he thought he'd need to make to pitchers over the course of the season, Ichiro said, **"When I get up to bat, I feel and get a sense of the pitcher. I analyze what he might throw me, then I trust my sense of the pitcher and make that adjustment. The more information I get on opposing pitchers, the better my performance may be. I can observe and use that. At the same time, opposing teams get more information on me."**

SEATTLE TIMES, May 22 2001

At the start of the season, Ichiro was asked which pitcher he was most eager to face. He immediately answered, **"Pedro [Martinez, of the Boston Red Sox]. He was with the major-league team that came to Japan in 1996, just before he became a superstar. I'm interested in seeing how much he's improved. And I want to see how much I've improved against him."**

SEATTLE POST-INTELLIGENCER, May 1 2001

Asked whether he thought he'd be able to make adjustments to pitchers over the course of the season, Ichiro said, **"The main point is that I have to learn the pitchers while I'm facing them now."**

NEW YORK TIMES, May 21 2001

Asked, during the off-season, whether he'd like to play with Alex Rodriguez, who was then considering whether to re-sign with the Mariners, Ichiro said, **"If I could play with Alex, that would be great for me, but as a human being, I understand he will make the best decision for himself, and I respect that."**

SEATTLE TIMES, November 30 2000

Referring to former Mariner Alex Rodriguez, Ichiro said, **"A-Rod told me not to get married before him, but I did. So maybe he got mad at me and left."**

SEATTLE TIMES, January 23 2001

Asked at the beginning of the season whether he felt any pressure to replace Alex Rodriguez, who left the Mariners for the Texas Rangers, Ichiro said, **"I'm not going to replace him. Rodriguez is an infielder and I'm an outfielder. He hits home runs and I don't. I just want the fans to like me for who I am."**

CANOE.CA, April 2 2001

In the Mariners' first game against former teammate Alex Rodriguez and the Texas Rangers, Ichiro hit safely 4 out of 6 times, including the game-winning home run in the 10th inning. Asked if he felt his performance had upstaged the confrontation between Rodriguez and his former team, Ichiro said, **"I don't ever want to upstage Alex. He's a wonderful player."**

SEATTLE POST-INTELLIGENCER, April 7 2001

Explaining why he wasn't yet performing at the level expected of him in spring training, Ichiro said, **"If I were in top condition on the first day, I'd be tired by the end of the season. I pace myself as the season goes on. By May and June, I get in a groove. That's my pattern. The month of April is a month of preparation. Maybe that doesn't sound good for the team, but it's the way I prepare. Then, as the season goes on, I get better."**

SEATTLE TIMES, May 22 2001

During spring training, the Mariners' hitting coach Gerald Perry said, "We'd like to get him to stop taking the early steps and drive the ball a little more before he runs." Ichiro said, **"It's often said that I do, but I do not run before I hit."**

WASHINGTON POST, April 29 2001;
TORONTO SUN, May 13 2001

"We're going to have Ichiro play in minor-league exhibition games," Piniella said. "He's not driving the ball or hitting it hard. Hopefully, that will cease. He needs to see a lot more live pitching, so we'll give him that opportunity." Piniella was heard wondering late in the spring: "Is that all he's got?" There was even some concern whether Ichiro was good enough to be an every-day player. Ichiro told several teammates, **"Wait until the season, then you'll see."**

SEATTLE TIMES, March 9 2001

During spring training, Ichiro was assigned to play for both sides in an intra-squad minor-league game, in order to lead off every inning and work on his bunting. He had 13 at-bats, going 6-for-12 – a home run, a double, and four singles, but no bunts. Asked why he didn't bunt, he said, **"They wouldn't throw me strikes."**

SEATTLE POST-INTELLIGENCER, March 28 2001

During spring training, Ichiro continued to hit nearly every ball to the left side and on the ground. Piniella said, "I couldn't just sit there and watch anymore. He just kept slapping the ball day after day. So finally I told him, 'Would you just pull the ball once? Just show me you can do it, will ya?'" Ichiro declined, saying, **"I'm just setting 'em up – no problem."** Mariners' left-fielder Al Martin, who overheard the conversation, said, "I couldn't believe he said that. Come on, nobody is that good. This isn't some Little League. You don't just walk into your first spring training, hang around everyone, and 'set people up.' I'm sorry – it doesn't work that way. He became a completely different player once the season started. You saw him drive the ball. You saw him slap the ball. You saw him do what the hell he wanted with the ball. I'd be lying if I thought he'd be anywhere near this good. I thought the best he'd do is get some cheap hits and pop the ball around. But this guy is good. I mean real, real good. I told him, 'I'm sorry. I was totally wrong about you. You are that good.'"

Piniella said he told Ichiro, "'Let's see if we can get you to hit to the pull field,' and today he did. It was an impressive day." Ichiro hit the ball hard to the right side for three singles. Afterward, Ichiro demurred, saying, **"I understand what the manager wanted to see, so I tried to show him, but then I got back to work, preparing for the season. This is the way I begin every spring, by hitting balls from center to left, to get my timing at the plate."**

SEATTLE TIMES, March 12 2001;
ESPN THE MAGAZINE, May 14 2001

After the spring-training game in which he got three base-hits to right field, Ichiro was asked whether he was pleased with the results. **"I learned a long time ago, whether I have a very good day or a very bad day, I never say it. You're better off letting others do that."**

SEATTLE TIMES, March 12 2001

ESPN commentator and former major-league pitcher Rob Dibble was so sure Ichiro would fail that he vowed to run naked through Times Square if Ichiro won the batting title; if Ichiro even batted .300, Dibble would strap on Speedos and make the same run. Informed that most analysts projected Ichiro hitting, at best, .280 in the major leagues, Ichiro, whose career average in Japan was .353, said, **"I don't understand where they come up with numbers like that. I don't know what they base it on. I'd love to know what the logic is."** On June 22, Ichiro was leading the American League in 11 offensive categories, including batting average (.356). Piniella told Dibble he "better start working on his tan."

WASHINGTON TIMES, June 10 2001;
SEATTLE POST-INTELLIGENCER, February 20 2001;
MARINERS BROADCAST ON FOX SPORTS NORTHWEST, June 22 2001;
SEATTLE POST-INTELLIGENCER, June 22 2001

Asked at the beginning of the season if he had any regrets leaving Japan to play in the United States, Ichiro said, **"I have no regrets following my dream to play in the major leagues. In fact, my only regret would have been if I didn't follow my dream."**

SEATTLE TIMES, January 23 2001

Asked whether he found it difficult to deal with the expectations that had been placed upon him as the first Japanese position-player to play in the major leagues, Ichiro said, **"In Japan, it was tough to play to the expectations everyone had. I don't want to be swayed by how the fans feel and how they expect me to play. One of the reasons I came over here is I wanted to find baseball was a fun sport."**

ESPN.com, March 21 2001

Asked if he came to the United States so that he could express his personality, Ichiro said, **"No, I expressed myself in Japan. That was never a problem. The reason I wanted to come here is because my fans wanted to see me take on a new challenge. Playing in Japan was not so interesting anymore."**

ESPNMAG.COM, May 2 2001

Asked what he had to say to Japanese fans who were disappointed that he was leaving the Japanese league for the major leagues, Ichiro said, **"My feelings about the fans who looked forward to seeing me play in Japan next season are complicated, but I hope if I have a chance to play in the majors next year, they will be happy for me."**

JAPAN ECONOMIC NEWSWIRE, October 12 2000

Asked whether he thought he'd have trouble
making the adjustment to the major leagues,
Ichiro said, **"Baseball is just baseball."**

SEATTLE POST-INTELLIGENCER, March 30 2001

Asked what was the most difficult adjustment
he has made so far, he said, **"I can't think of
anything, so there must not be anything."**

MLB.com, May 30 2001

When the Mariners played against the Red Sox, Ichiro was asked what his reaction was to being the first Japanese position-player to bat against a Japanese pitcher, Hideo Nomo, in the major leagues. **"I see him only as one of the opponents,"** Ichiro said. **"And I think he looks at me the same way."**

BOSTON GLOBE, May 3 2001

Before facing Boston Red Sox pitcher Hideo Nomo–which was treated by media in Japan and America as an event of geopolitical significance: the first time a Japanese position-player had batted against a Japanese pitcher in the major leagues–Ichiro said, **"Everyone says this is a Japanese player against a Japanese player. Hopefully, that talk has died down."**

BOSTON GLOBE, May 8 2001

When the Mariners played against the
Red Sox in May, Ichiro was hit in the back on
a pitch by Hideo Nomo. Asked whether Nomo
was attempting to send him a message, Ichiro
said, **"I don't imagine this is the first hit-by-pitch done by a Japanese pitcher in major
league baseball."**

SEATTLE POST-INTELLIGENCER, May 3 2001

Ichiro's bunt single catalyzed the Mariners' 5-4 victory in the first game of the season, and Japanese reliever Kazuhiro Sasaki saved the game. Asked if he thought all of Japan was celebrating, Ichiro said, **"I can't speak for all Japanese people, but I'm sure there's some celebrating going on."**

SEATTLE TIMES, April 3 2001

When Ichiro said that he would not be going to see the movie *Pearl Harbor*, a reporter asked him if this was because he found the subject matter objectionable. Ichiro explained that, in order to keep his vision sharp, **"I can't sit and watch anything that is long, such as a movie, any movie."**

SEATTLE TIMES, May 26 2001

Asked what he'd miss about Japanese baseball, Ichiro said, **"There is nothing I will miss about Japanese baseball. Off the field, I will miss my dog, but nothing on the field."**

SEATTLE POST-INTELLIGENCER, March 30 2001

Asked his dog's name, Ichiro said, **"I would not wish to say without first asking its permission."**

SPORTS ILLUSTRATED, May 28 2001

Appearing on a local talk-show and asked to give Seattle a pre-season message, Ichiro said, in English, **"Hey, Seattle, what's up?"**

JAPAN TIMES, January 18 2001

During spring training, Ichiro said that he was trying to learn one word of English every day. **"The only problem,"** he said, **"is that I learn a word, but I go to bed, and by the time I wake up, I've forgotten it, so the next day I have to start over."** Asked what word he had learned today, he said, **"It was a bad word, so I can't say what it was."**

SEATTLE POST-INTELLIGENCER, February 21 2001

Ichiro explained that he is picking up bits and pieces of English by listening to television, movies, and hip-hop. **"I very much like hip-hop,"** he said.

SPORTS ILLUSTRATED, May 28 2001

Explaining why, in contrast to his teammate, Kazuhiro Sasaki, Ichiro prefers not to have a translator on call next to him in the locker room, he said, **"When we have team meetings, I need a translator, but I try to get by on my own in the clubhouse. When the guys are joking around, even though I don't understand all the words, I can feel what's going on."**

ESPN THE MAGAZINE, May 2001

Trying on his new uniform during spring training,
Ichiro was unhappy with how baggy the pants
were. Edgar Martinez, the Mariners' beefy
All-Star designated hitter, said, "Bueno, bueno."
Ichiro replied, **"No bueno."**

SEATTLE POST-INTELLIGENCER, February 21 2001

Piniella came up to Ichiro around the batting
cage and asked him how everything was going.
"Muy bueno," he replied.

BASEBALL WEEKLY, May 30 2001

Asked what has been the biggest adjustment he's had to make, Ichiro said, **"I'm eating a lot more pizza for lunch than I'm used to."**

ASAHI SHIMBUN, May 8 2001

Asked what he eats on the road – for instance, in Arlington, Texas, where there aren't many Japanese restaurants – he said, **"I actually ordered a steak at a sports bar there. And it was pretty good, especially for a sports bar."**

MLB.com, May 30 2001

Asked how he feels that so many fans from Japan appear to have voted for him for the All-Star team, Ichiro said, **"I'm very pleased that they're interested in major league baseball and the All-Star Game, rather than the number of votes."**

"MARINER TALK" ON KIRO, June 18 2001

Asked in mid-June how he feels about four Mariners being the leading American League vote-getters at their positions for the All-Star Game in Seattle — Bret Boone, Edgar Martinez, John Olerud, and himself — Ichiro said, **"Maybe except me, the other players are very deserving to get such a huge number of votes. If and when I'm selected with my teammates, I'll be very honored and very happy to play with them in Seattle."**

"MARINER TALK" ON KIRO, June 18 2001

Asked whether he was gratified to receive the most votes of any player for the All-Star game, Ichiro said, **"We the players play baseball for ourselves. At the same time, the fans are so pleased to see me playing the game, I'm starting to change my feeling. They've been so nice to me I now like to play for them."**

"MARINER TALK" ON **KIRO,** June 18 2001

On Ichiro Suzuki Day, the day before Opening Day, Ichiro said, **"I was surprised to feel how cold it was when I arrived in Seattle, but after two [exhibition] games here in Safeco Field, I felt the warmth from you fans, and it was the same warmth that I felt in Arizona."**

NORTHWEST ASIAN WEEKLY, April 5 2001

Asked what he likes most about playing baseball in the United States, Ichiro said, **"I like the fans. I like the attitude they take to baseball. Their passion as fans is very high."**

ESPNMAG.COM, May 7 2001

Asked why he thought some fans in other ballparks had reacted negatively to him the first month of the season, Ichiro said, **"You'll have to ask the fans. I just try to play hard every day. I don't really care what the fans at away games say about me."**

ASAHI SHIMBUN, May 8 2001

Asked to compare Japanese fans to American fans, Ichiro said, **"The fans cheer in Japan, but it's more organized than it is here. In Japan, it's 'Three-two-one, Ichiro!' Here, it's more spontaneous. When I play well, they applaud and I can feel their support. It happens more naturally here and that makes me happy."**

MLB.com, May 30 2001

"I love how the Mariners really function
together as a team," Ichiro said. "That feeling
is important to me."

ASAHI SHIMBUN, May 8 2001

Told that his 19-game hitting streak tied for the season's best in the American League and asked for his reaction, Ichiro said, **"I wouldn't have known if you didn't tell me."**

TORONTO SUN, May 14 2001

After getting a base hit in 22 consecutive games, Ichiro was asked whether he thinks much about keeping the streak alive. He said, **"This being the age of information and technology, it's inevitable to know that kind of stuff through media people, but I'd rather simply play baseball day in and day out. In a game situation, I don't think about it when I hit. It's not my goal. After I get a hit, I don't say, 'Oh, I got another one.'"**

LOS ANGELES TIMES, May 18 2001

Asked for his reaction to his 23-game hitting streak coming to an end, Ichiro said, **"Please don't think about the streak too hard. Someday it's going to be over and today's the day it's over."**

DENVER POST, May 21 2001

Asked if he was disappointed that his 23-game hitting streak had come to an end, Ichiro said, **"I always try to play hard, but today I didn't get the results. I don't have any regrets or shame, because I tried as hard as possible."**

SEATTLE TIMES, May 20 2001

In the game in which Ichiro's hitting streak came to an end, Yankee pitcher Orlando Hernandez hit Ichiro in the back with a pitch in the eighth inning. Asked whether he thought Hernandez hit him on purpose, thus denying Ichiro what would have been his last opportunity to get a hit if the game hadn't gone into extra innings, Ichiro said, **"Don't ask me that question."**

DENVER POST, May 21 2001

Summarizing the lesson he learned from his slump in 1999, Ichiro said, **"Failure is the mother of success."**

ICHIRO AND THE INTERVIEW: ATTACK THE PINNACLE!, April 2001

Ichiro was asked how he would compare the 23-game hitting streak he accomplished in the major leagues to the two 23-game hitting streaks he accomplished in Japan's Pacific League. **"That was a long time ago,"** he said. **"I don't remember how I felt then, so I can't compare the two."**

SEATTLE POST-INTELLIGENCER, May 18 2001

Ichiro, asked what he thought his batting average would be in his first major-league season, said, **"I honestly have no idea what I'll hit. I never set personal statistical goals. All I want to do is play to the best of my ability."**

SEATTLE TIMES, March 30 2001

Although he's right-handed in every other way, Ichiro bats left-handed, which allows him to get to first base a crucial step faster than batting right-handed would. Asked how or why he came to bat left-handed, he said, **"I just always hit that way and have no memory why."**

MLB.com, May 30 2001

Ted Heid, the Pacific Rim scout and part-time translator for the Mariners, said, "Ichiro's intelligence is off the charts." Asked by a reporter whether he did well in school, Ichiro said, **"I did well in school until junior-high. I studied hard, got great marks. Then I went to high school. After I went to high school, all I did was baseball and sleeping."**

SEATTLE TIMES, February 21 2001

When asked what he would like to do on an off day, Ichiro answered, **"I want to watch American kids playing baseball on a grass field, running around, and getting hoarse in the voice with my wife."**

ICHIRO AND THE INTERVIEW: ATTACK THE PINNACLE!, April 2001

Asked how he handles the pressure from fans and media to succeed in the United States, Ichiro said, **"I don't play baseball for other people. I play baseball for myself. They can put whatever pressure they want to put on you, but I don't feel it. I really don't have any idea what they are expecting me to do. I just play the best I can."**

SEATTLE TIMES, March 30 2001

Ichiro told a reporter, "They say you are successful in baseball if you only fail 70 percent of the time, that going 3-for-10 is successful. As long as I play, I will look for a way to improve on that. If a pitcher beats me 7 of 10 times, I can accept that. But if I get myself out in some of those at-bats, that I can improve on. In this game, there's something every day you can be disappointed with…. The biggest adjustment has been that in Japan, the tempo of a pitcher was like 1-2-and-3. Here, it's more 1-2-3, with no 'and,' so I had to find the way to take the 'and' out of my swing to match that tempo. I did it by changing the stride with my front foot. It was enough. I cannot be satisfied with a number, because it may not reflect how you did. If you set a goal, achieving it may satisfy you and you won't try to go beyond that goal. Every at-bat, there's something to learn from, something to improve. It's in the seeking that you find satisfaction."

TACOMA NEWS TRIBUNE, May 8 2001

Asked how his first month in the major leagues
had gone, Ichiro said, **"I'm really enjoying myself
and learning something every day."**

ASAHI SHIMBUN, May 8 2001

Discussing his adjustment from Japanese baseball to American baseball, Ichiro said, **"It can be hard. Every day is something new. You have to study everything, but I like this very much."**

WASHINGTON POST, April 29 2001

When Ichiro visited a Seattle grammar school and was asked by students for advice, he said, **"Find something you like to do as soon as possible."**

SEATTLE TIMES, May 20 2001

While visiting the grammar school, Ichiro said, **"I don't know whether I'm going to be a baseball player in ten years, but I hope I can see you in the future."**

SEATTLE TIMES, June 1 2001